Original title:
Mole Hills and Moonlight

Copyright © 2024 Swan Charm Publishing
All rights reserved.

Editor: Jessica Elisabeth Luik
Author: Olivia Orav
ISBN HARDBACK: 978-9916-86-182-0
ISBN PAPERBACK: 978-9916-86-183-7

Lifting Shadows

Whispers in the twilight air,
Silent secrets softly share,
Beneath the moon's gentle gaze,
Night unfolds in shadowed haze.

Stars alight the sky so grand,
Sprinkling light on darkened land,
Echoes of the past arise,
Through the veil of midnight skies.

In the stillness, shadows lift,
Casting dreams as darkness drifts,
Moments lost to time's embrace,
Found again in starlit grace.

Pagodas Beneath Stars

Pagodas rise in twilight glow,
Silent sentinels in row,
Underneath the starry veil,
Tales of old their stones regale.

Moonlight dances on the eaves,
Whispers weave through ancient leaves,
Mysteries from eras past,
In the starlight's gentle cast.

Serenity in night's embrace,
Heaven's glow on earthly place,
Pagodas stand in tranquil light,
Guardians of the peaceful night.

Dappled Dreams

In the meadow, sunlight beams,
Painting hues in dappled dreams,
Whispers of the wind's soft song,
Where the hearts of dreamers long.

Blossoms sway with gentle grace,
Petals smile in sunlit space,
Silent symphony of peace,
In the day's serene release.

Golden rays through shadows play,
Promises of a brighter day,
Lost in reverie so deep,
Wondrous visions while we sleep.

Quiet Crests

Waves of silence slowly crest,
Lulled by whispers, hushed to rest,
In the stillness, softly kiss,
Moments of pure peacefulness.

Moon's embrace on tranquil sea,
Harmony in quiet spree,
Melodies of night's soft breath,
Serenades that conquer death.

Drift in dreams on gentle tide,
Calm and peace so deep and wide,
Quiet crests in night's caress,
Held in nature's soft finesse.

Sublime Nocturne

Stars stitched in velvet skies,
Dreams whisper in soft sighs.
Moon's glow tenderly woos,
Night's symphony renews.

Owls serenade the dark,
Wings spread, a secret mark.
Crickets weave lullabies,
Echoes of nature's ties.

Silver mists gently rise,
Dew reflects starlit eyes.
A hush embraces all,
As constellations call.

Blood of the Earth

Ancient roots delve below,
Crimson rivers in flow.
Mountains stand tall and proud,
Nature's anthem, unbowed.

Rustling leaves tell a tale,
Of winds that moan and wail.
Seasons etch earth's wisdom,
Unseen, a realm of phantoms.

Forest shadows convene,
Guardians of the green.
Whispers of time unseen,
Breathe life, unseen machine.

Subtle Night Elevation

Gentle breezes arise,
Caressing the night's guise.
Darkness, subtle embrace,
Woven in sable lace.

Mountains touched by moonlight,
Eclipsing day's eyesight.
Secrets held in silence,
Beyond the day's pretense.

Stars, like whispers, glitter,
In night's expansive theater.
Heightened senses align,
With cosmic, silent sign.

Veiled Illumination

Midnight cloaks the landscape,
Shadow realms under drape.
Silver whispers entwine,
With moon's soft, tender shine.

Secrets hide in shadows,
Beneath moon's pale hallows.
Veils of dark, softly part,
Revealing night's pure art.

Lanterns cast mellow light,
Piercing the heart of night.
Ephemeral and bright,
Guiding through endless night.

Twilight Rises

The sky ignites in amber hues,
A whispered glow of day's adieu.
Shadows stretch as night ensues,
Stars emerge in velvet blue.

In silence, crickets serenade,
The world in twilight softly fades.
Breezes cool the sunlit glade,
Nighttime's calm in dark cascades.

Owl hoots echo through the night,
Moonbeams cast their silver light.
Rest we find, in dreams take flight,
'Til dawn's first break, a soft invite.

Enigmatic Crests

Mountains rise in misty shrouds,
Echoes lost in ancient crowds.
Mysteries in the rocks endowed,
Whispers of the past avowed.

Winds that whisper secrets old,
Tales of courage, hearts so bold.
Legends in the heights unfold,
Enigmatic crests behold.

Lonely peaks in azure skies,
Gaze upon with timeless eyes.
Journey to the height implies,
Truths beyond what earth comprise.

Celestial Trellis

Stars entwine in cosmic dance,
A trellis of the night's expanse.
Galaxies in vast romance,
Eternal in their shimmering trance.

Nebulae in colored bloom,
Swirl within the deep night's doom.
Planets round in silent room,
Orbit through the endless gloom.

Meteor trails in brief delight,
Blaze across the velvet night.
Witnesses in distant light,
Guardians of the sky's great height.

Climbing Under Stars

Up we go through twilight's veil,
Bound by dreams that never fail.
Trailing moon, our loyal sail,
Climbing under stars so pale.

Hand in hand, we trace the bends,
Path unseen but till it ends.
Each step closer to transcend,
Hearts aglow on heights depend.

In the hush of night we strive,
Bound by love, our spirits thrive.
Underneath the stars, alive,
Together in the sky we dive.

Celestial Digging

In the vast expanse, we dig with light,
Piercing through the cosmic night.

Stars like diamonds, hidden deep,
In the sky's eternal keep.

Galaxies swirl, mysteries unfold,
Tales of creation candidly told.

Nebulae whisper secrets old,
Hints of stories yet untold.

Through the void, our journey grand,
Exploring wonders vast and unplanned.

Silent Celestial Dialogues

Planets converse in silent tone,
In a language all their own.

Moons orbit with gentle grace,
Silent dancers in cosmic space.

Comets carve paths bold and bright,
Messengers in the endless night.

Asteroids drift, wanderers free,
Whispers crossing the cosmic sea.

In the silence, the stars confide,
Celestial dialogues side by side.

Whispers of the Night

The night whispers secrets low,
To the heart it starts to show.

Dreams that drift on moonlit breeze,
In the stillness, souls find ease.

Stars above, they softly hum,
To the beat of a cosmic drum.

Silent echoes of the past,
Through the night, forever cast.

Each whisper holds a silent thrill,
A promise that the night fulfills.

Small Rises

A sprout breaks through the morning dew,
Reaching for the skies so blue.

Tiny wings on the first flight,
Chasing dreams with all their might.

A heartbeat finds its steady beat,
In life's rhythm, soft and sweet.

Small rises bring a gentle sway,
Marking the dawn of a new day.

With courage small and tender heart,
Every journey makes its start.

Big Dreams

Eyes closed, mind takes flight,
On wings of dreams, into the night.

Visions grand in the vast unknown,
A world of wonder to call their own.

Chasing stars, grasping light,
Turning shadows into bright.

Hopes that rise on silent beams,
Crafting worlds from fragile dreams.

In the heart, ambition streams,
Boundless as the endless dreams.

Hidden Lights

In the depths of ancient nights,
Whispers brush the silent trees.
Hidden lights in shadows play,
Guiding souls on secret breeze.

Silent moons cast their glow,
Over lands that dream in rest.
Secrets in the dark unfold,
Mysteries that glow the best.

In the heart of twilight's veil,
Glimmers of a lost past show.
Hidden lights lead the way,
Where the quiet rivers flow.

Below the Velvet Sky

Below the velvet sky so grand,
Stars like jewels brightly stand.
Moonlight weaves a silver thread,
Dreams are born where night is spread.

Constellations brightly gleam,
Painting tales in astral stream.
Whispering winds of yesternight,
Carry hearts to new delight.

Softly sings the night's lullaby,
Cradles earth from high up nigh.
Below the velvet sky's embrace,
Life's mysteries we beautifully trace.

Earth's Nightly Embrace

When shadows stretch across the land,
And twilight paints with gentle hand,
Earth's nightly embrace unfolds,
In the secrets that night holds.

Forests sway in night's calm hymn,
Stars emerge at twilight's rim.
Echoes of the day's retreat,
Whisper night's enchanting beat.

Cool as dew on morning's grace,
Night wraps earth in its embrace.
Dreams take flight in starry dance,
In the hush of night's expanse.

Craters and Shadows

On the moon's pale, dust-kissed face,
Craters hold their silent place.
Shadows stretch in haunting grace,
Marking time's unending race.

Lunar seas in silent rows,
Lifetime scars the surface shows.
Stars above in endless gaze,
Illuminate the moon's old ways.

In the stillness of the night,
Craters stand by shadow's light.
Tracing stories long and vast,
In the moonlight's gentle cast.

Veins of the Night

Stars thread through the fabric
of dusk's flowing embrace.
Veins of the night whisper
of dreams left in trace.

Shadowed paths beckon us,
through silence and time.
Heartbeats sync with shadows,
creating a silent rhyme.

Midnight whispers secrets
only the night can unveil.
A world of hidden wonders
beneath the moon's pale.

In the quiet of the night,
an enchanting spell is spun.
Veins of the night pulsate,
promising secrets yet to come.

Moonlit Passageways

Under the silver gaze,
we wander and we roam.
Moonlit passageways call,
beckoning us home.

Soft glows lead us onward,
a journey through the night.
Each step a silent story,
under the moon's light.

Whispers of the breezes,
sing in hushed tones.
Moonlit passageways carve paths
through fields of unknowns.

Guided by the silver,
we traverse through dreams.
Each path a moonlit promise,
more than it seems.

Subterranean Reflections

Beneath the world above,
a realm of shadows play.
Subterranean whispers
reflect a hidden day.

Caves echo lost voices,
their ripples in the dark.
Subterranean reflections
leave a fleeting mark.

Ancient stones hold stories,
etched in timeless lore.
Every subterranean corner,
teems with tales of yore.

Lost in these deep halls,
we find a mirrored hue.
Subterranean reflections
of worlds both old and new.

Night's Gentle Excavation

As dusk falls to twilight,
the night begins its delve.
Gently excavating,
into dreams we selves.

Unearthing from the past,
fragments of old light.
Night's gentle excavation
reveals memories bright.

Silence in the uncovering,
a tapestry unfolds.
Delicate the night's hands,
pulling threads of gold.

Each star a silent witness
to the night's quiet quest.
Excavating dreams and time,
laying shadows to rest.

Hidden Beneath the Surface

In quiet depths where secrets sleep,
Whispered tales of shadows deep,
Mysteries woven by time's own hand,
Under currents of silken sand.

In twilight's glow, unseen, unheard,
Life unfolds without a word,
Beneath the waves, in silent grace,
An unseen world, a hidden place.

Fragments of light, dancing in play,
Stars reflected in the bay,
Unveiling stories long concealed,
By ocean's breath, gently revealed.

Through the Veil of Dusk

As twilight drapes its velvet shawl,
Night's embrace begins to call,
Shadows stretch in evening's loom,
Crafting wonders from the gloom.

Stars awake in silent hymn,
Eyes aglow where light grows dim,
Through this veil, a world anew,
Painted soft in shades of blue.

Secrets shared by moonlight's kiss,
Whispered dreams in moments' bliss,
Dusk unveils the night's domain,
Hearts alight within its reign.

Stardust on Earth

Stars have journeyed far and wide,
Scattered dust in cosmic tide,
Their essence mingled with our own,
In mortal form, their presence shown.

In every breath, a piece of sky,
Woven dreams where spirits fly,
Footprints made with stardust grace,
Echoes of a stellar place.

Galaxies in every glance,
Mystic dances, cosmic trance,
On this Earth, a link we share,
With the universe, beyond compare.

Of Earth and Ether

From soil's embrace to sky's expanse,
Life's rhythm in a timeless dance,
Roots dig deep while spirits climb,
Blending mortal with the sublime.

In every leaf, a story spun,
Of earth and air and setting sun,
Boundless ether, grounding soil,
Intertwined in nature's toil.

Harmony in every breath,
Bridge between life and death,
Of Earth and Ether, seamless we,
Merge as one in unity.

Ridge Lines in Nightfall

Dusky veils over mountains sweep,
As stars ignite night's canvas deep,
Whispers of winds in valleys weep,
Ridge lines in nightfall secrets keep.

Horizon fades in twilight's glow,
Shadowed hues in quiet flow,
Moonlight etches peaks below,
In night's embrace, the ridges grow.

Crisp air carries echoes clear,
Of silence reigning, drawing near,
Across the range, the night sincere,
Ridge lines paint dreams austere.

Serenade of Peaks

Heights where eagles serenade,
Echoes of their calls cascade,
Peaks in rendezvous displayed,
Night descends, their song portrayed.

Skyward spires in moon's accord,
Silent hymns the stars afford,
Mountains vast, a nature's chord,
In darkness, peace and light restored.

Slumbered trees in whispers sing,
Their branches to the stars they cling,
On lofty trails the spirits spring,
Serenade of peaks, night's offering.

Twinkling Ascents

Tracks of light through night's ascent,
Stars align in firmament,
Mountains rise in shadows bent,
Twinkling paths, where dreams are sent.

Glistening trails that starlight guide,
Climbing high where hearts reside,
Celestial rivers open wide,
In twilight's arms, the mountains abide.

Journey's end where sky and peaks,
In twilight languages it speaks,
Twinkling whispers through the creaks,
Ascents glowing, the calm it seeks.

Hidden Brilliance

Mountains guard their mystic glow,
In twilight's grasp, their secrets flow,
Veiled in night, their colors show,
Hidden brilliance in shadows sow.

Silent nights, the stars parade,
On peaks where gentlest dreams invade,
Veins of light in dark conveyed,
Brilliance hidden, softly laid.

Mysterious contours edged in light,
A dance with darkness every night,
Mountains in their quiet might,
Hidden brilliance, a tranquil sight.

Hushed Elevations

Whispers climb the silent peak,
Stars behold the muted dance.
Valleys yawn and shadows speak,
Mountains weave their astral trance.

Snowflakes kiss the weathered stone,
Eagles trace their timeless path.
Nature's hymn, a sacred tone,
Echoes in the aftermath.

Moonlight drapes the sleeping trees,
Breezes hum their gentle song.
Harmony in twilight's ease,
Where the lofty dreams belong.

Clouds embrace the twilight's hue,
Ridges hold the twilight's grace.
Night unfolds the skies anew,
In this hallowed, tender place.

Unearthed Radiance

Golden beams through soil and earth,
Unseen roots that seek the light.
Secrets hidden find their birth,
In the dawn that ends the night.

Raindrops feed the thirsty ground,
Life awakes in colors bright.
Nature's rhythm, soft and sound,
Guides the bloom to reach its height.

Sunlit whispers brush the leaves,
Morning's glow in petals' fold.
Each new bud that daylight weaves,
Tells a story yet untold.

Crystals glint in morning's gaze,
Choruses of life arise.
Nature's gem, in light's embrace,
Beneath the vast and endless skies.

Lifted Echoes

Voices ride the twilight breeze,
Songs of old in whispers found.
Through the branches, past the seas,
Echoes lift from sacred ground.

Melodies on wings take flight,
Binding hearts with unseen thread.
In the dark or in the light,
Harmonies the breeze has spread.

Choruses of times gone by,
Sung by wind and whispered streams.
Lifted echoes, soaring high,
Woven deep in nature's dreams.

Every note a timeless tale,
Every rhythm, ancient lore.
Songs of earth and sky detail,
Echoes lifted evermore.

Eve's Alchemy

Dusk descends in golden hues,
Transmuting day to night.
Stars emerge in twilight's muse,
Filling skies with silver light.

Mystic potions in the air,
Blend the sun with moon's embrace.
Alchemist with tender care,
Changes scenes with gentle grace.

Twilight's magic, soft as lace,
Weaves a spell of evening's charms.
Nighttime's warmth and sweet embrace,
Held in quiet twilight arms.

Silent whispers hold the key,
Secrets of the fading sun.
In the heart of eve's alchemy,
Day and night become as one.

Pebbles and Starlight

By the shore, where dreams take flight,
Pebbles shine in soft moonlight.
Waves whisper secrets, tender and slight,
Under the canvas of a tranquil night.

Stars above in twinkling delight,
Guiding souls through darkest plight.
Hearts are bound in the shimmering light,
As pebbles twinkle, pure and bright.

Time flows gently, out of sight,
Each pebble's edge a testament slight.
To the universe, vast and tight,
In endless wonder, hearts unite.

Subtle Heights

In silent woods, where whispers lean,
Mountains rise in shades unseen.
Echoes of dreams in valley's sheen,
Subtle heights, so serene.

Every peak a tale untold,
Winds of courage, ages old.
Graceful mists in morning gold,
Untamed spirit, bold.

Silent paths where shadows sleep,
Climbing toward the heavens deep.
With each step, a promise to keep,
Subtle heights, memories reap.

Ethereal Glow

In twilight's embrace, where shadows play,
An ethereal glow begins to sway.
Soft hues of dawn in tranquil array,
Guiding seekers on their way.

Gentle whispers of evening's close,
In the breeze, a tender prose.
As night unfolds and softly shows,
The magic within an eternal rose.

Under the stars, where wishes lie,
The ethereal glow fills the sky.
Dreams awaken, hearts comply,
To the night's soft, lullaby.

Hidden Peaks

Beyond the veil of morning mist,
Lie hidden peaks, by sunlight kissed.
Mysteries echo, in twilight's tryst,
Nature's wonders, quietly persist.

Paths untraveled, whispers concealed,
In each step, a secret revealed.
Mountains' hearts, so well-heeled,
Hidden peaks, memories sealed.

In the distance, shadows grow,
Guiding spirits in realms below.
With silent grace, onward they go,
Toward the peaks, where dreams flow.

Gently Lifted

Soft whispers in the morning dew,
Where sunlight kisses skies anew.
Breezes gentle, day unfolding,
Nature's stories, softly molding.

Petals blushing, morning greeted,
Songs of dawn, all worries retreated.
Quiet moments, heartstrings lifted,
In the stillness, gifts are gifted.

Forgotten dreams find gentle voices,
In the hush, the world rejoices.
Each new color, softly knitted,
In the calm, our spirits lifted.

Memories in the winds are snared,
In the silence, hearts are bared.
Tender moments, softly shifted,
By nature's grace, gently lifted.

Silhouetted Curves

In twilight hour, shadows throng,
Elegant lines, a silent song.
Moonlight dances, dreams unfurled,
In the silence, another world.

Curves of night in gentle sweep,
In the dark, desires sleep.
Silver hues on surface cast,
Etched in time, shadows last.

Underneath the evening's shade,
Where time and space both gently fade.
Contours whisper, softly laid,
In dusky light, secrets played.

Hidden tales in shadows spun,
Where light and dark together run.
Silhouetted, softly blurs,
A dance of dreams, in twilight stirs.

Enchanted Dust

In the stillness, dawn breaks clean,
Shimmering light, a tranquil scene.
Suspended pearls in morning trust,
Softly touched by enchanted dust.

Whispers carried on the breeze,
Mystic tales between the trees.
Glimmering sparkles, spirits sing,
Nature's whispers on gossamer wing.

Paths of gold in twilight kissed,
By the fabled, unseen mist.
Step by step, each heartbeat's trust,
Guided softly by enchanted dust.

Serene sighs in midnight's glow,
Magic spins where dreams do flow.
In every particle, stories thrust,
Breathes the world, enchanted dust.

Crescent Casts

In the quiet, night unfurls,
A crescent moon in silver swirls.
Casting shadows, dreams amassed,
Where the night's own spells are cast.

Stars in millions, silent waltz,
Light and dark in soft repulse.
Underneath the sky's vast blast,
Mystic tales in crescent cast.

Through the window, shadows creep,
Whispers softly, lulling sleep.
In their dance, dreams intertwined,
Wonders in the dark aligned.

Through the night, the crescent sails,
Weaving through the midnight veils.
In the dark, the moments last,
By the moon's own crescent cast.

Under the Quiet Night

Whispers of the moon, soft and mild,
A lullaby sung for the lonely child,
Stars above in silent delight,
Guide the weary through the night.

Beneath the skies, shadows dance,
In a trance, they intertwine and prance,
Heartbeats echo, tender and light,
In harmony under the quiet night.

Veils of time, dusk to dawn,
Mysteries whispered, then swiftly gone,
In this stillness, pure and bright,
Dreams take flight under the quiet night.

Starlit Burrows

Deep within the earth's embrace,
Lie caverns filled with timeless grace,
Underneath a sky of endless blues,
Stretch the paths of starlit burrows.

Glimmering gems in the hidden dark,
Whispers of the ancient mark,
Echoes of a universe so close,
Shimmer softly in starlit burrows.

Secrets of the deep unfold,
Under ceilings crafted bold,
Mysteries that time bestows,
Live and breathe in starlit burrows.

Burrowed by Nightfall

As twilight bends to evening's call,
Shadows stretch across the hall,
Creatures move with silent thrall,
In chambers burrowed by nightfall.

Echoes of the day retreat,
Leaving behind a hushed heartbeat,
In the soil, secrets sprawl,
Among paths burrowed by nightfall.

Moonlight streams through tiny holes,
Casting threads of silver scrolls,
Magic lies in each earthen wall,
In the nooks burrowed by nightfall.

Radiance Below

Hidden worlds beneath our feet,
Where silent wonders quietly meet,
Lanterns glow with amber's hew,
Illuminating the radiance below.

Crystals sparkle in the gloom,
Turning midnight into bloom,
Every corner starts to glow,
Revealing the radiance below.

Footsteps echo soft and slow,
Through caverns where the secrets flow,
In the earth, a subtle show,
Of nature's radiant below.

Mystic Shadows

In twilight's warm embrace, they creep,
Where silence reigns, the secrets keep,
Whispers of the night so deep,
Mystic shadows, dreams in sleep.

Veiled in silver, moonlit flame,
Ancient tales that have no name,
Through the darkened woods, they came,
Mystic shadows, none to blame.

Dancing on the edge of light,
Echoes of a bygone night,
Guarding mysteries out of sight,
Mystic shadows, fleeting flight.

Soft whispers in the autumn breeze,
Stirring leaves 'neath ancient trees,
Carving paths no eye yet sees,
Mystic shadows, gentle tease.

In the quiet, they confide,
Where the worlds of dreams collide,
Mystery, their only guide,
Mystic shadows, side by side.

Somber Heights

High upon the mournful peaks,
Where the silent sorrow speaks,
Lonely echoes, timeless weeks,
Somber heights, the soul it seeks.

Gray and solemn, skies are veiled,
Through the mists, the heart has sailed,
Every tear-streaked path detailed,
Somber heights, where love has failed.

Whispers of forgotten days,
Lost in twilight's gentle haze,
Echoes sing in mournful praise,
Somber heights, in muted gaze.

Winds that moan through ancient stone,
Chilled as if to marrow, bone,
Silent as a whispered tone,
Somber heights, forever known.

In the distance, shadows fall,
Voice of time, an endless call,
Nature answers, great and small,
Somber heights, where spirits thrall.

Luminescent Grid

City lights like stars below,
Through the veins, their currents flow,
Mapping dreams where few dare go,
Luminescent grid aglow.

Neon rivers chase the night,
Guiding souls through dark and light,
Flickers blink, a transient sight,
Luminescent grid so bright.

Paths entwine in gleaming threads,
Promise of what lies ahead,
Endless stories left unread,
Luminescent grid widespread.

In the hum of urban song,
Where the heartbeats move along,
In the glimmer, we belong,
Luminescent grid stands strong.

When the world lies dark and still,
Streetlights cast their magic spell,
Dreams emerge that fate can't quell,
Luminescent grid, farewell.

Dusky Epitome

When the sun begins its fall,
Casting shadows long and tall,
Hushed twilight, a whispered call,
Dusky epitome of all.

Crimson skies in twilight's blaze,
Final dance of fading rays,
Day and night in soft embrace,
Dusky epitome, a place.

Stars awaken, one by one,
As the day's last light is done,
Silent witness to the sun,
Dusky epitome begun.

Whispers in the cooling air,
Evening's breath with tender care,
Secrets shared with those who dare,
Dusky epitome so fair.

In this moment, time stands still,
Promises the night will fill,
Peace descends, the world to thrill,
Dusky epitome's gentle will.

Nocturnal Whispers

In the silence of the night,
The whispers gently flow,
Through moonlit beams so bright,
In dreams they softly grow.

Beneath the starry glaze,
A secret lullaby,
Whispers form a maze,
In night's embrace they lie.

The owls' hollow call,
Echoes through the dark,
A shadow on the wall,
Whispers leave their mark.

In quietude so deep,
The night begins to weave,
Whispers while we sleep,
Our fears they do relieve.

Roots Among Stars

Among the cosmic dust,
Our roots begin to sprawl,
In stardust we find trust,
The universe our hall.

Celestial vines entwine,
From earth to distant light,
In space they intertwine,
Roots glowing in the night.

Through blackened voids they climb,
Seeking light so far,
Bound by endless time,
Roots among the stars.

Galaxies they feed,
With ancient, silent power,
In constellations freed,
Roots bloom a stellar flower.

Dusk's Quiet Footsteps

As daylight starts to wane,
The shadows gently creep,
Dusk's quiet footsteps reign,
Over fields that fall asleep.

A tranquil hush descends,
On the weary day,
As twilight blends and bends,
In dusk's soft, muted sway.

Leaves whisper secrets low,
In the fading light,
Footsteps wandering slow,
Mark the coming night.

With steps so softly laid,
Dusk binds earth and skies,
In this woven shade,
To dreams our spirits rise.

Underground Luminescence

Beneath the earthy crust,
In caverns dark and deep,
A glow of gentle trust,
In shadows softly seep.

Mushrooms bathe in light,
Of luminescent hue,
In the eternal night,
A secret world anew.

Crystals catch the gleam,
Reflecting ancient tales,
In the quiet gleam,
Where time itself pales.

Among the roots, there lies,
A glow that never fades,
Underground it sighs,
In whispering cascades.

Whispers in the Soil

Beneath the layers, ancient tales unfurl,
Silent murmurs from the core unfurl.
Roots like fingers weaving through the years,
Earthbound secrets whispering in ears.

Seeds of yore, embedded with a dream,
Gardens sprout where sunlight gleams.
Time and weather carve the silent ground,
Among the whispers, life is found.

Each pebble holds a million voices past,
Every grain a story, forever cast.
Silent though they seem, they softly sing,
Of yesterdays and what tomorrow brings.

Underfoot, a world unknown to light,
Mysteries written in the dark of night.
Whispers quiet, yet they reach the soul,
In the soil's hush, we are whole.

Nocturnal Glow

Moonlight dances on the midnight floor,
Casting shadows through the open door.
Stars like lanterns hung in velvet skies,
Reflecting dreams in our heavy eyes.

Fireflies paint whispers in the air,
With their small glows, a gentle flare.
Night's embrace, a soft, alluring sight,
Guides us gently through the quiet night.

Leaves rustle, silken in the breeze,
Branches sway like ships upon the seas.
Glowworms sketch their luminescent streams,
Paths enlightened by our twilight dreams.

Crickets serenade the silver sheet,
Nature's ballad, rhythmic and sweet.
In the heart of night's tranquil flow,
We bask within its soft, nocturnal glow.

Nights Between the Crickets

Silent night, yet teeming life calls,
Between the crickets, a symphony enthralls.
Rhythmic chirps, a language so clear,
Nature's conversations, we hold dear.

Underneath the stars' celestial play,
Crickets sing in orchestral array.
A chorus echoing in the in-between,
In the spaces, hidden worlds are seen.

By brook and meadow, voices blend,
In twilight's grasp, these songs transcend.
Each pause a breath, a sigh of connection,
In cricket-filled nights, a serene reflection.

In dark's embrace, we find our tune,
Guided softly by the crickets' croon.
Nights alive with their whispered lanes,
In between the crickets, peace remains.

Beneath the Starlit Canopy

Underneath the starlit canopy,
Time suspends in eternity.
Galaxies spiraled in cosmic dance,
We find solace in their glance.

Leaves weave shadows on earthly veil,
Stars tell stories in night's pale.
Every twinkle, a whispering lore,
In the starlit canopy, we explore.

Wind's soft caress through the grass,
Celestial lights in their silent mass.
The universe in hushed dialogue,
Guides our souls through midnight fog.

Beneath the expansive sky so wide,
Hearts and dreams no longer hide.
In cosmic embrace, we are free,
Bound by the starlit canopy.

Slight Ascents

On the path of slight ascents,
Where the whispering winds do play,
I find solace in the silence,
As night turns into day.

Leaves fall in gentle patterns,
Painting scenes of peace and grace,
Mountains loom in soft surrender,
Their peaks a warm embrace.

Stars ignite the tranquil evening,
Lighting paths we often dread,
Walking onwards with conviction,
To the dreams that lie ahead.

Time, a patient guide, reminds us,
Of the heights we're yet to seek,
In each moment lies an echo,
Of a future still to speak.

Through the mists of slight ascents,
Every step a whispered song,
In the journey lies our power,
To the ever-right the wrong.

Night's Gentle Touch

When the sun bids its farewell,
And the stars embrace the night,
A calm descends, a soft expanse,
Bathed in silver light.

Whispers of the cool, crisp air,
Caress the weary soul,
In Night's gentle, tender touch,
We find ourselves whole.

Luna's glow upon the streams,
A mirror to the skies,
Reflecting dreams in quiet realms,
Where peace and stillness lie.

Hushed is the song of twilight,
Crickets in sweet refrain,
Lulling thoughts to softer dreams,
Until dawn breaks again.

Embrace the night, its gentle touch,
Let worries gently fade,
For in the starlit silence found,
Our fears are all allayed.

Soft Horizon Lift

Upon the soft horizon lift,
Where dawn meets tender hues,
The world awakens slowly,
In pastel shades and blues.

Clouds drift in a lazy dance,
Kissed by the morning's breath,
Whispers of a day reborn,
From night's embrace of death.

Ripples on a waiting sea,
Reflect the sky's embrace,
Bringing with each soft caress,
A sense of timeless grace.

Birdsong heralds day's ascent,
A hymn of hope and light,
Carried on the winds of change,
From darkest depths of night.

In the soft horizon's lift,
Beyond our worldly cares,
We find the strength to start anew,
As morning gently dares.

Mystic Twinkles

In the canvas of the night,
Lie mystic twinkles far and near,
Each a spark of untold wonders,
In the sky so vast and clear.

Constellations tell their stories,
Ancient riddles in the dark,
Guiding hearts with timeless wisdom,
Lighting up the soul's own spark.

Eyes that search the starry blanket,
Find solace and delight,
In the mysteries unfolding,
With each tiny, twinkling light.

Dreams are woven in the ether,
On the loom of midnight's thread,
Binding hopes and silent whispers,
Of the living and the dead.

In the secrecy of twilight,
Where wishes dare to gleam,
Mystic twinkles hold our yearnings,
In the heart of every dream.

Earthen Stars

In fields where wildflowers gleam,
Under skies that softly beam,
Dwell the stars of earthly gleam,
In a universe of dream.

Grass whispers tales to the night,
Crickets sing their pure delight,
Moon in shadows casts her light,
Earthen stars, a wondrous sight.

Rivers dance with liquid ease,
Wind-song rustles through the trees,
Nature's magic here to seize,
Peaceful days and evenings' breeze.

Mountains watch with ancient eyes,
Silent under starlit skies,
Lonely wolves in distance cries,
Echo through the night that flies.

Morning's blush will come again,
Signing earth with dew-kissed pen,
Until then, my humble pen,
Writes of stars in earthen glen.

Midnight's Embrace

Shadows fall with gentle grace,
As we meet in midnight's space,
Stars ignite the darkened face,
Of the night we both embrace.

Whispers float through silent air,
Moonlight drapes you, silken care,
Dreams unfold with tender flare,
In this realm where hearts lay bare.

Softly tread the paths we know,
Silent winds begin to blow,
Guiding steps where love will show,
In the midnight's mellow glow.

Timeless moments, firmly sown,
Weave a tapestry unknown,
In your eyes, a love has grown,
Under stars, together, shown.

Dawn will come to break this spell,
But the night has tales to tell,
In our hearts where whispers dwell,
Midnight's song will always swell.

Serene Ascendancies

Hills that climb towards the skies,
Cloaked in misty morning highs,
Whispers of the dawn arise,
Silent, pure, and gentle sighs.

Cresting waves of golden hue,
Sunlight breaks with purpose true,
In the green, the world's anew,
Bathed in endless, wondrous view.

Eagles cast their shadows wide,
O'er the valleys, soaring, glide,
Freedom found on every side,
In the air and far and wide.

Tranquil streams in valleys flow,
Carving paths where dreams may grow,
Deep within the earth below,
Life ascends in ebb and flow.

Here, the soul can find its space,
In the nature's warm embrace,
Elevations, pure with grace,
Rising in this peaceful place.

Illumined Nightlines

City's glow in darkness shines,
Tracing out the skyline's lines,
Here where urban beauty twines,
In these quiet midnight times.

Neon lights and silent streets,
Humming with the night's heartbeats,
Passing moments no one greets,
On a path where calmness meets.

Windows glare with inner light,
Stories hidden out of sight,
Each a tale of silent might,
In the tapestry of night.

Cars pass by in steady streams,
Underneath the starlit beams,
In the stillness of the dreams,
Life is more than what it seems.

Morning comes with tender glow,
Illuminating all we know,
But the night lines softly flow,
In the city's quiet show.

Starlit Mounds

Upon the hills, where shadows crest,
Beneath the moon, our hearts invest.
The night adorns the silent sound,
In starlit dreams, our souls are bound.

The sky a canvas, dark yet bright,
Each star a candle in the night.
Mountains hum with whispers found,
Echoes dance on starlit mounds.

A chill of night, yet warmth inside,
Beneath the heavens, worlds collide.
With every step, the stars astound,
We traverse the starlit mounds.

Quiet Luminescence

In hush of night, the world lays still,
With gentle glow upon the hill.
Whispers of the moon's soft light,
Guide us through the quiet night.

Each leaf and stone, a story tells,
Beneath the stars, enchantment dwells.
A touch of magic, pure and bright,
Unveils the night's soft, quiet plight.

Through velvet skies, the silence flows,
In every breeze, the cosmos knows.
In night's embrace, we find our essence,
Wrapped within its quiet luminescence.

Slopes Under Silver

Beneath the silver moon's embrace,
The slopes reveal a tranquil grace.
Each shadow cast, a silent thrill,
Through silver light, the night is still.

A realm where dreams and stars align,
In silver folds, we intertwine.
With every breath, the mountains shiver,
In the glow of silver's quiver.

The slopes, a canvas pure and fair,
Where night and light are aptly paired.
A world unspoken, calm yet clever,
We walk the slopes under silver.

Glistening Undulations

Waves of light in twilight's fold,
Stories in the silence told.
Hills that shimmer, gently swayed,
In glistening undulations, played.

Each rise and dip, a dance so grand,
Beneath the stars, by night's command.
Soft ripples through the twilight land,
Glistening waves on silver sand.

A melody of light and lands,
In night's embrace, the heart expands.
On gentle slopes, our path we trace,
In glistening undulations' grace.

Underworld Dreams

In shadows deep where whispers play,
The night unfolds its hidden way,
A symphony of silent screams,
We wander through underworld dreams.

The moon's soft glow like phantom's breath,
Guides us through the void of death,
A realm unseen by mortal eyes,
Where truth and dark illusion lies.

Veiled figures dance in eerie light,
Their forms obscured in endless night,
We glide like ghosts through ashen streams,
Entwined within our underworld dreams.

Ancient echoes fill the air,
With memories forgotten, rare,
A labyrinth of times and seams,
We're lost inside these chilling dreams.

When dawn arrives, will we be free,
From whispered vows and ghostly plea,
Or will we find, through night's extremes,
We're bound to our underworld dreams.

Twilight's Soft Secrets

When day meets night in gentle hush,
The sky adorned with twilight's blush,
Soft secrets here begin to tell,
In whispers sweet, the dusk's farewell.

Stars appear, a quiet choir,
Lit by the sun's last fading fire,
They sing of realms, both near and far,
As twilight weaves its silent char.

The trees lean in, their shadows cast,
On breaths of wind, the moments pass,
Each leaf a tale on twilight breeze,
Of dreams afloat on midnight seas.

An owl's call breaks the tender air,
A song of dusk, a night's affair,
The moon ascends, a watchful eye,
Over secrets hid in twilight sky.

As darkness fills the world anew,
The stars confess, their stories true,
And so we drift, within the net,
Of twilight's soft secrets we've met.

Echoes of the Tunnels

Through winding paths and walls of stone,
The whispers fly, we're not alone,
Each step we take, a timeless trace,
In echoes of this hidden place.

The air is thick with tales untold,
Of lives entwined, of hearts grown cold,
Their voices linger, soft and pale,
Within the tunnels where they wail.

A lantern's light, a flicker's dance,
Reveals the past with every glance,
Here shadows speak in muffled tones,
Of labyrinths as cold as bones.

Lost souls entwine in endless quest,
For answers cloaked within their rest,
Their hopes and fears, like ghostly mists,
Within these tunnels they persist.

Yet if we listen, hearts attuned,
To whispers from the darkened rune,
We too may find our own deep calls,
Within the echoes of these halls.

Luminous Nightscape

Underneath the starry dome,
Where night's embrace feels like a home,
The world glows with a gentle grace,
A luminous nightscape we embrace.

The moonlit path through silent trees,
A silver thread on midnight's breeze,
Each step a dance, each breath a song,
In night's vast canvas, we belong.

The constellations, stories bright,
Adorn the blanket of the night,
They guide our thoughts, our dreams alight,
In countless sparkles, pure and white.

Beneath this sky, our worries fade,
In soothing shadows night has made,
We're cradled by the velvet dark,
Each star a pixel, each a spark.

In this serene and quiet space,
We find our peace, a soft embrace,
The world, a luminous expanse,
Invites us in its silent dance.

Midnight's Embrace

Under the cloak of darkened skies,
Whispers of dreams softly arise,
Stars sprinkle tales in cosmic lace,
Wrapped in midnight's tender embrace.

Moonbeams dance on velvet night,
Echoes of the heart take flight,
Shadows weave a mystic space,
Bound by midnight's gentle grace.

Silence hums life's hidden tune,
Cradled by the watchful moon,
Twilight's end a sweet solace,
Lost in midnight's warm embrace.

Secrets bloom from tranquil hush,
In the stillness, hearts do rush,
Night bestows a calm, slow pace,
Nestled in midnight's sweet embrace.

Pulled by the Tides

Whispering to the restless shore,
Oceans sing forevermore,
Waves that rise and then subside,
Pulled by the endless, longing tide.

Moonlit waters, silver-bright,
Hold the secrets of the night,
Currents swell with force and pride,
Pulled by the ebbs of ancient tides.

Seashell whispers haunt the breeze,
Mysteries call from beneath deep seas,
Sailors' hearts, adrift, collide,
Pulled by the ocean's yearning tide.

Pulsing waves of oceans wide,
Timed to lunar cycles, guide,
In this dance, a world implied,
Pulled by the grand, unyielding tide.

Luminous Elevations

Mountains bathed in morning light,
Kissed by dawn with hues so bright,
Peaks that pierce the sky's great veil,
Luminous heights in sunrise pale.

Whispers of the winds up high,
Carry dreams to touch the sky,
Ridge by ridge, the earth's grand tale,
Luminous peaks where hearts prevail.

Streams of sunlight, gold they trace,
Nature's art in silent grace,
Valleys deep where shadows fall,
Luminous summits standing tall.

Through the mists and ancient stones,
Mountains hum with whispered tones,
Reaching where the skies unveil,
Luminous heights that never fail.

Secret Nocturnes

Whispers soft in dark night's keep,
Stars awash in cosmic deep,
Moon's glow sifts through dreams' allure,
Sung in nocturnes, pure and sure.

Silhouettes of sighs and beams,
Draped in twilight's mystic seams,
Echoed murmurs softly purr,
In the night's veiled overture.

Crickets sing their lullaby,
To the stars who greet the sky,
In the cool, dark night's obscure,
Secret songs of time secure.

Dreams unfurl with wings so wide,
In the night, they gently glide,
Tales spun in shadowed contour,
In twilight's secret nocturnes pure.

Beneath the Celestial Veil

Stars whisper secrets in the night,
Through the sky, they dance with light,
Lost in dreams, we take flight,
Beneath the celestial veil.

Moonbeams bathe the earth in glow,
Shadows waltz with whispers low,
In this realm, we ebb and flow,
Beneath the celestial veil.

Galaxies spin in silent grace,
Countless worlds in timeless space,
We journey to an endless place,
Beneath the celestial veil.

Comets blaze their fleeting trail,
Waves of wonder without fail,
Together, we set our sail,
Beneath the celestial veil.

In the stillness of the night,
Magic lives in purest sight,
Our spirits soar in boundless flight,
Beneath the celestial veil.

Silvered Darkness

In the hush of twilight's breath,
Moonlight leads the dance of death,
Silent whispers, icy wreath,
Silvered darkness takes its hold.

Shadows creep with tendrils long,
In the night, we find our song,
Murmured secrets, whispered wrong,
Silvered darkness, deep and bold.

Stars cry out in muted grief,
Veiled in night, there's no relief,
We trace sorrow's fragile leaf,
Silvered darkness, ghostly cold.

Whispers linger, tales of old,
Through the gloom, the truth is told,
Hearts entwined in silver fold,
Silvered darkness, tales unfold.

Peace emerges from the night,
Gently kissed by silver light,
In the shadows, dreams take flight,
Silvered darkness, pure delight.

Digging through Dreams

In the garden of our minds,
Buried deep, the treasure finds,
Digging through, what fate unwinds,
Dreams revealed in slumbered land.

Layers thick with years of toil,
Hidden truths beneath the soil,
Secrets bloom in midnight's oil,
Dreams arise with gentle hand.

Through the mist of hazy night,
Visions come, a second sight,
In the darkness, purest light,
Dreams unfold in whispered strand.

Memories weave with present thread,
In the tapestry we're led,
By the dreams that we have fed,
Futures rise from waking sand.

In our hearts, where shadows play,
Digging deep, we find our say,
Dreams that guide us on our way,
In the night, where hopes expand.

Nocturne of the Burrows

In the dark, the creatures hide,
Burrowed deep, their secret ride,
Through the night, with dreams as guide,
Nocturne sings the burrowed way.

Quiet hums of hidden lives,
Underneath, what peace derives,
In the shadows, spirit thrives,
Nocturne whispers, come to stay.

Softly tread where silence reigns,
In the heart, where stillness gains,
Life beneath the earth's domains,
Nocturne hums the gentle strains.

In the depths where dreams align,
Silent stories intertwine,
Souls converge in perfect sign,
Nocturne croons the stars' design.

Safety found in earthen nest,
Dreams of night bring needed rest,
In the burrows, we are blessed,
Nocturne's song, our hearts caressed.

Roots and Radiance

Beneath the ancient oak, roots intertwine,
Drawing whispers from the earth's design.
Sunlight dapples leaves with golden trance,
In the forest's heart, nature's secret dance.

Silent strength, beneath, in darkness deep,
Where stones whisper secrets they keep.
Roots grasp soil with relentless might,
Feeding dreams of the forest's light.

Branches stretch against the azure sky,
Leaves flutter, on breezes they fly.
In reverence, the flora bows below,
To the light, where radiance flows.

Sunset paints the heavens in hues of gold,
A story of light that never grows old.
Night descends, with gentle calm,
Cradling the forest in nature's palm.

By dawn's first light, the cycle resumes,
Roots and radiance, in silent blooms.
Nourishing life, as shadows fade,
Nature's bond, forever made.

Midnight's Soil

Under the cloak of midnight's tress,
The soil breathes a timeless caress.
Whispering tales of ancient lore,
In the darkness, mysteries explore.

Stars above, in silent gleam,
Reflect in puddles, a night's dream.
Owls call through the silent veil,
Echoing tales from shadowed trail.

Moonlight filters through shadowed trees,
Dancing with leaves on a midnight breeze.
Silent whispers of things unseen,
In the soil's embrace, where dreams convene.

Roots delve deep in the earth's embrace,
Binding time in this sacred place.
Glimmers of life in hidden toil,
Unfolding secrets in midnight's soil.

In silence lies the echo of day,
Tucked in the soil, where shadows play.
Midnight stands, a quiet sentinel,
Guarding the soil, where dreams dwell.

Silent Excavations

Beneath the surface, in quiet repose,
Lies a world where the unseen grows.
Silent excavations, with careful hand,
Reveal the secrets of this ancient land.

Bones and fossils, relics of time,
Stories buried in the soil's rhyme.
Unspoken histories lie in wait,
For gentle touch to excavate.

Archaeologists with hearts of care,
Uncover whispers hidden there.
Fragments pieced with patient grace,
Reviving echoes from time's embrace.

Silent dust, from eras long past,
Reveals the shadows that forever last.
Brushing gently, with reverent mind,
Finding truth in the soil's grind.

In careful pause, earth's past speaks,
Of civilizations that history seeks.
Silent excavations, tenderly,
Bring the ancient world to you and me.

Earthbound Epiphanies

Walking through fields of emerald green,
Wonder's whisper lies unseen.
In every leaf and blade of grass,
Earthbound epiphanies come to pass.

Clouds drift in a sky of boundless blue,
Nature's canvas in constant view.
Whispers of wisdom in the breeze,
From the branches of ancient trees.

Sunlight kisses the dewdrop's gleam,
Each spark a fragment of a dream.
Earth's embrace, with gentle sway,
Guides the soul on its wandering way.

Mountains rise with solemn grace,
Peaks that touch the celestial space.
In the valley, life unfurls anew,
Earth's epiphanies in every hue.

Standing still, with eyes closed tight,
Absorbing nature's quiet light.
Revelation in the earthy air,
Epiphanies whisper everywhere.

Twilight Contours

Shadows stretch in twilight's embrace,
Gentle whispers fill the space.
Daylight fades, a tranquil hue,
Stars ignite in night's soft view.

Dusk descends on silent wings,
Nature in a soft choir sings.
Contours blur in the fading light,
Dreams awaken with the night.

Crickets serenade the moon,
Owls call an eerie tune.
Mountains bask in twilight's kiss,
A moment of ethereal bliss.

Paths unknown in shadows lie,
Secrets whispered by the sky.
Peace envelops land and shore,
In twilight's tend, forevermore.

Horizon melts in hues of gold,
Stories of the dusk unfold.
Calm resides in twilight's flare,
Nighttime's delicate affair.

Soft Beams

Morning dew on tender leaves,
Sunlight dances, gently weaves.
Soft beams caress the sleepy land,
A warm touch by nature's hand.

Golden rays through the windows creep,
Awakening the world from sleep.
Birdsong weaves with sunlight's tune,
Dawn awakens far too soon.

Glimmering in the early light,
Fields of green in radiant sight.
Soft beams bless each budding flower,
Heralding a quiet hour.

Whispers of a new day's start,
Painting joy in every heart.
Soft beams guide as shadows flee,
In the morning's tranquil plea.

The world aglow in gentle beams,
Wrapped within the daylight's dreams.
Harmony in golden streams,
Soft beams unite in sunlit themes.

Glimpses in the Gloom

Silent night and whispers near,
Softened sounds, no need to fear.
Glimpses in the twilight's cloak,
Where mysteries and shadows soak.

Fireflies in gentle flight,
Dots of hope within the night.
Glimpses through the shadows seen,
Magic in the dark serene.

Moonlight dances on the pond,
In the gloom, a hidden bond.
Glimpses of the stars above,
Weave a tale of quiet love.

Voices hushed by night's embrace,
Secrets told in shadowed space.
Glimpses caught through midnight's veil,
Whispering a timeless tale.

Glimmers in the velvety dark,
Stars ignite with gentle spark.
In the gloom, where stillness blooms,
Glimpses weave enchanting rooms.

Gentle Slopes

Rolling hills in daylight's grace,
Gentle slopes, a serene place.
Grass sways in the warm-breathed breeze,
Nature's lullaby through the trees.

Sunlight kisses meadows wide,
Butterflies in graceful glide.
Gentle slopes where cattle roam,
Canvas of Earth's fertile home.

Soft ascent of verdant green,
Peaceful, pastoral, and serene.
Gentle slopes in twilight's gleam,
Awake the heart, inspire the dream.

Whispered winds on gentle plains,
Softly waltz in summer rains.
Gentle slopes where rivers wind,
In nature's lap, solace find.

Fields stretch out in endless peace,
Embraced by hills with sweet release.
Gentle slopes, a soothing see,
Tranquility in green decree.

Veiled Horizons

Beneath the twilight's muted haze,
Where shadows stretch in silent praise,
The horizon hides its tender grace,
In veils of night, it finds its place.

Whispers linger on the breeze,
Through ancient branches of the trees,
A promise of what's yet to be,
In twilight's calm, the heart is free.

Stars emerge in silver streams,
Casting light on secret dreams,
A world unseen, beyond our schemes,
Where time flows slow, or so it seems.

Distant echoes softly call,
In the stillness of nightfall,
Veiled horizons, after all,
Hold mysteries that both rise and sprawl.

Subdued Radiance

In the dawn's first quiet light,
Softly breaking through the night,
Subdued radiance takes its flight,
Painting skies with hues so bright.

The world awakens slow and sweet,
To the rhythm of its heartbeat,
Golden rays in silence greet,
The day begins, life feels complete.

Through the morning mist and dew,
A tender glow in shades of blue,
Nature's palette, ever true,
Whispers secrets old and new.

Paths of light and shadow play,
In the early break of day,
Subdued radiance finds its way,
Guiding dreams where they may stray.

Silvan Nocturne

In the forest, dark and deep,
Where ancient secrets gently keep,
A silvan nocturne stirs from sleep,
In twilight's arms, shadows seep.

Moonlight dances through the leaves,
Weaving patterns twilight weaves,
An ethereal light, nature grieves,
For lost moments the heart perceives.

Owl's serenade cuts through the night,
Echoes of their silent flight,
Melodies of pure delight,
In this woodland bathed in light.

Whispers in the midnight air,
Tell tales of creatures, swift and rare,
In this nocturne, free from care,
The forest breathes, its soul laid bare.

Silvered Ascent

Upon the mountain's silent crest,
Where eagles make their lofty nest,
A silvered ascent, we are blessed,
With views that set the soul at rest.

Mist and moon in soft embrace,
Paint the peaks with tender grace,
A tranquil, timeless, sacred space,
Where hearts and minds find their place.

The stars above in silent glow,
Witness to the world below,
In their light, our spirits grow,
Guided by what they bestow.

Through the night, the path unfolds,
Silver trails through silent holds,
In the ascent, our dreams are bold,
Seeking truths the heart enfolds.

Small Worlds

In gardens where small flowers bloom,
A hidden life takes root and grows.
Among the petals, worlds assume,
The beauty only silence knows.

Ants and beetles, unseen hosts,
Carry on their tiny quests.
Each leaf and blade, their posts,
A microcosm never rests.

Raindrops fall, a gentle sea,
Rippling through an emerald land.
Tiny treasures, wild and free,
Within the grasp of nature's hand.

Sunlight dances, shadows play,
On fields of green and golden skies.
In these small worlds, life holds sway,
Beneath our unassuming eyes.

Big Shadows

In twilight's hush, the shadows grow,
Stretching long across the vale.
Silent whispers in their flow,
Echo tales, ancient and frail.

Trees like giants, stark and tall,
Cast their secrets on the ground.
In their shade, the shadows call,
With a voice, profound and round.

Mountains loom in dusk's embrace,
Their silhouettes, a bold decree.
Shadows speak of hidden grace,
In a language wild and free.

The moon alights upon the scene,
Drawing shapes with silver light.
Big shadows in a world serene,
Guarding secrets of the night.

Midnight's Gentle Embrace

Stars adorn the velvet sky,
In midnight's gentle sweet embrace.
Whispers soft as dreams pass by,
Night's calm touch, a tender grace.

The moon, a beacon pale and grand,
Guides the weary hearts to rest.
In its light, we understand,
The night's embrace, a loving guest.

Owls call with haunting voice,
Through the silence, pure and deep.
In their song, a sacred choice,
Midnight's secrets, still we keep.

Dreamers drift on tides of night,
To lands where fantasies awake.
In midnight's tender, soothing light,
Gentle hearts can mend, not break.

Roots in the Dark

Deep within the forest's heart,
Where shadows weave a hidden dance.
Roots in the dark, their secrets part,
Bind the earth in firm expanse.

Mysteries lie beneath our feet,
In soil where ancient memories keep.
Roots entwine in silence sweet,
Hold the stories in their deep.

Trees above, with branches wide,
Reach for sunlight, pure and bright.
Yet roots in darkness, side by side,
Draw their strength away from sight.

In the shadowed world below,
Where life begins and whispers grow.
Roots in the dark forever show,
The silent pulse all beings know.

Celestial Silver

Celestial silver, moonlit beams,
Adorn the night with quiet grace.
In the dark, where silence dreams,
Stars awaken in their place.

A sky aglow with twinkling light,
Guides the weary through the night.
Each silver thread, a gentle sight,
Woven into midnight's flight.

Planets spin in silent dance,
Through the cosmos, vast and free.
Celestial silver, many a glance,
Offers whispers of mystery.

Eternal glow of galaxies,
In endless space, a timeless sea.
Celestial silver carries these,
Echoes of infinity.

Hillocks and Radiance

On hillocks green with morning light,
The whispers of the dawn take flight,
Sunlit beams kiss morning dew,
Turning every leaf anew.

A sea of grass that gently sways,
Under skies that burn ablaze,
With nature's song so pure and clear,
Each note a fondly whispered cheer.

Emerald waves and golden gleam,
Life's a softly flowing stream,
With every crest a tale unwinds,
Of ancient lore and new designs.

Mountains watch with ageless grace,
Their stolid faces soft embrace,
The endless dance of day and night,
In radiant hues, a pure delight.

A world that's wrapped in light and shade,
Where fleeting moments gently fade,
Into a canvas vast and wide,
Each stroke a story's gentle guide.

Glow of Dusk

The sky adorned in twilight's hue,
With orange, gold, and violet too,
The sinking sun bids its adieu,
To stars that wish the night anew.

Shadows stretch as night draws near,
Soft whispers float, no longer clear,
The world transforms in dusky light,
In soft embrace of coming night.

Lanterns flicker in the breeze,
Amongst the rustling of the trees,
Footsteps fade on cobblestone,
As night prepares its gentle throne.

A hush descends on busy streets,
As daylight's fervor now retreats,
Moonlight's glow, both calm and bright,
Paints the world in black and white.

The glow of dusk, a fleeting dance,
In tender, tranquil, fierce romance,
A fleeting glance of time's soft hand,
A quiet spell cast o'er the land.

Stardust and Earth

Beneath a sky of diamond's gaze,
The earth abides in silent praise,
For each celestial light does sing,
Of mysteries the night doth bring.

Stardust drifts on midnight's breeze,
Lands on leaves and ancient trees,
Glimmers on the ocean's crest,
Whispers of a cosmic quest.

In fields where wildflowers bloom,
Their petals shine in starry plume,
Blessed by light from distant places,
Bridging all the vast, dark spaces.

The earth and stars, a timeless link,
From cosmos wide to night's deep brink,
A dance that never sees an end,
A bond that seasons won't transcend.

Through telescope or naked eye,
The endless depths of starry sky,
Invite the heart to ponder worth,
Of fleeting life 'twixt stardust, earth.

Night's Peaks

High atop night's lofty peaks,
The moonlight whispers, softly speaks,
To valleys deep and shadows long,
A tender, melancholy song.

Crested heights in twilight glow,
Where winds of ancient stories blow,
And secrets kept by time's own hand,
Are scattered 'cross the starlit land.

Stars align in silent grace,
Marking paths in vast, dark space,
A journey traced by dreamer's sight,
Guided by the arc of night.

Mountains bathed in silver sheen,
Stand as keepers of the scene,
From dusk till dawn they hold their guard,
With secrets written, skyward starred.

Night's peaks bear witness old and wise,
To the dance of worlds and skies,
In their shadows, truth does sleep,
In their heights, the cosmos weep.

Milton Keynes UK
Ingram Content Group UK Ltd.
UKHW050809240724
445899UK00013B/460